Allen & Mike's Really Cool
TELEMARK
TIPS

109 amazing tips to improve your tele-skiing

Allen O'Bannon
&
Mike Clelland!

A FALCON GUIDE ®

Falcon® Publishing is continually expanding its list of recreation guidebooks. All books include detailed descriptions, accurate maps, and all the information necessary for enjoyable trips. You can order extra copies of this book and get information and prices for other Falcon® guidebooks by writing Falcon, P.O. Box 1718, Helena, MT 59624 or calling toll free 1-800-582-2665. Also, please ask for a free copy of our current catalog. Visit our web site at http://www.falconguide.com

1 2 3 4 5 6 7 8 9 0 TP 03 02 01 00 99 98

Falcon and FalconGuide are registered trademarks of Falcon® Publishing, Inc.

All photos by authors unless otherwise noted.
Cover illustration by Mike Clelland.

Congress Cataloging-in-Publication Data
Clelland, Mike.
    Allen and Mike's really cool telemark tips / by Mike Clelland and Allen O'Bannon.
        p.   cm. — (A Falcon guide)
    ISBN 1-56044-851-2 (pbk. : alk. paper)
    1. Telemark (Skiing) I. O'Bannon, Allen. II. Title.
  III. Title: Telemark tips. IV. Series.
GV854.9.T44C54 1998
796.93—dc21   98-42639
                                                CIP

CAUTION

Outdoor recreational activities are by their very nature potentially hazardous. All participants in such activities must assume the responsibility for their own actions and safety. The information contained in this guidebook cannot replace sound judgment and good decision-making skills, which help reduce risk exposure, nor does the scope of this book allow for disclosure of all the potential hazards and risks involved in such activities.

Learn as much as possible about the outdoor recreational activities in which you participate, prepare for the unexpected, and be cautious. The reward will be a safer and more enjoyable experience.

♻ Text pages printed on recycled paper.

Contents

Acknowledgments

This is a list of the floppy-heeled friends who contributed to this book:

Rich "Agro-C" Rinaldi, Clair "Sneaky" Yost, Don "The Steeps" Sharaf, Chris "Riding Porpoises" Lander, K. K. "Toy Train" Cool Day, Erika "Punch Downhill" Eschholz, Jim Ferguson, Margaret "Ski the Trees" Thompson, Mitch "I'd rather be climbing" Ross, Angela "Knees Together" Patnode, Bill "Equal Weight" Morewinkel, Tracy Jane "The Right Equipment" Young, Mark Johnson, Tony Jewell, Deb Payne, Tori Hederman, Brad Sawtell, Molly "Tray" Absolon, , Kristn "Unweight" McInaney, Christian Beckwith, Mark Bergstrom, Nina Cook, Greg Collins, Willy "Turn Faster" Peebottle, Marc Kessler, Sarah Levesen, Bill "Butt Cheeks" Zell, Matt Mitchel, Mindy Breen, Jeff Newsome, Lynn "Bounce" Morrison, Andy "Bouncy Bouncy" Wallbert, some lady from New Hampshire, Connely "3rd Dimension" Brown, Cotton T-shirt Ned, Brien "How to Fall" Sheedy, everbody at the NOLS Idaho winterbase, and all the other powder hounds that drop the knee and not the bomb.

A word from Mike!

I ain't no great skier. There are millions of tele-skiers out there that're lots better than me. The fact is, I'm not a natural athlete; it's only through ten years of hard work that I've gotten to the point I'm at today. I'm not really a ski instructor, either. I do work for an outdoor school a few weeks each winter, but mostly we teach winter camping, not telemarking.

What I am is a cartoonist and ski bum. My formative years were spent reading MAD magazine and now I'm forever incapable of seeing things normally. There are some curious and bizarre implications to a youth spent doodling. My brain simply doesn't work like other people's. (Just ask Allen.) In this book I've worked hard to transpose the subtle mechanics of telemark skiing into an overtly visual and berserk cartoon-a-rama. My goal was to give you something concrete to latch onto in the midst of all these sometimes esoteric skiing skills.

You'll probably notice my editorializing in these drawings. I like to get low in my turn, I prefer the backcountry to chairlifts, I like powder, and I ski on leather boots. One advantage to leather boots, from my point of view, is that they're easier to draw than plastic boots. Similarly, mittens are easier to draw than gloves. Gaiters make the calves look skinnier so you can better see the stance. All telemarkers require a woolly Peruvian llama-herder hat with ear flaps, and no illustration is complete without some drips of sweat and "Boiing" marks. I hope these drawings make it clear that I love to ski!

But please don't get all high-and-mighty and serious about this book. These cartoons are meant to convey some helpful hints in an extremely caricatured way, which means that there ain't nothing subtle here! Don't think you're some kind of a smarty-pants just because you spot some little flaw in the technique of these cartoon skiers. The value of the drawings (I hope) is that they provide an easy-to-remember visual hook that'll help you put these tips to use. Please enjoy this book.

Enough said,

Mike!

A word from Allen

This book is our attempt to help you improve your skiing. I must admit that originally I was skeptical about the idea of writing a ski tips book—not because I didn't think it would be fun or useful (or because I didn't think we would achieve fame and fortune), but rather because skiing is such a hard thing to teach. One person's key to success doesn't work for someone else—often because that someone else is too busy struggling with some uncooperative part of their anatomy to comprehend the valuable advice just given them. It's all they can do to respond "uh-huh."

The key to learning a dynamic sport like skiing is to spend a lot of time on skis. As instructors, we try to give folks tips on what they should do next, based on where they're at in their skill development. But lets face it: If you're not ready for a particular tip, then all you really want to do is spend time on your skis and keep your butt off the snow. Once in awhile, though, we manage to give someone the right tip at just the right time, and off they go—totally satisfied and shredding at a new level. And that's what teaching is all about.

So I figured if we just filled this book with a variety of tips that worked for a variety of people, we might come up with something useful—not just for beginning and intermediate skiers, but also for some of those burnt-out instructors who are in need of some fresh air. And aside from all that, I knew that with Mike's illustrations, the book would at the very least be entertaining.

I learned to telemark at the advanced age of twenty-three, and I've taught telemarking for the past ten years. Through this experience I have come to realize that there are two basic fundamentals hopeful free-heelers must master. The first is maintaining balance while moving. Anyone can stand still on one leg, but to do it while moving is a different story, and mastering this skill takes some of us longer than others. The best way to get the dynamic balance required is to simply spend time on skis gliding about. You don't necessarily need to be doing turns downhill; just kicking and gliding along in the flats will help. Indeed, I try to convince my students to spend as much time as possible on their skis, because the more comfortable you are with those long pointy things on your feet, the better you will be at controlling them.

The second fundamental is maintaining the correct body position. It is virtually impossible to telemark if all your body can do is stand up straight. You need to be able to bend those knees and drop into those turns! Practice holding this position while doing straight runs on mellow terrain, and eventually some muscle memory will kick in. You can spice up this routine by switching lead skis as you are moving, and by bending even further at the knees to see how low you can go.

If you are new to skiing, you may want to start out on the packed slopes of a ski area rather than in the backcountry. The packed snow will make it easier to concentrate on the basics, and the lift service will allow you much more time to work on your downhill technique.

A.O.

1 Use this book

This book isn't designed to languish on your coffee table or on your bookshelf, it's meant to be used! Put it in your pack and bring it along with you when you're skiing. You'll notice this book is nothing more than a bunch of little tips meant to help you improve your skiing, so don't expect it to give you much of a step-by-step progression into the turn. (We'll leave that to Paul Parker's excellent book.) Rather, you should flip through this book and find those tips most relevant to you. Study the ones that you like and then practice, practice, practice! There's also a section at the end of the book that points out some common mistakes; this section will guide you to the tips that will help you correct these mistakes. So if any of these problems seem painfully familiar, simply turn to the appropriate tip for help. And, oh yeah, don't forget to have fun!

apply proper **THUMB** pressure

2 Review the border cartoon

The little flip-art cartoon along the book's border shows a pretty darned accurate tele-skier rippin' it up. Use this as a learning tool. As you improve, all you need to do is flip the pages faster to quicken up the rhythm, just like real life.

3 Floppy heels vs. locked-down

Are you coming from a background of alpine skiing? Do you want to learn the telemark turn? If so, get ready to be a beginner all over again. (Good for the soul.) This isn't a rule, but some of the most frustrated skiers you see are lifelong alpine skiers trying to telemark for the first time. These folks are locked into a specific muscle memory that can be disastrous when applied to tele-gear. There are some fundamental differences between the alpine and telemark turn, and there are pros and cons to each. If you feel that alpine skiing is getting a little stale and you're ready to evolve, free-heel gear may be just the challenge you're looking for. There is a certain freedom to having a floppy heel. The main advantage is that you can travel beyond the limitations of the lift-served resorts. Free your heel, your soul will follow.

Some tele-facts:

- You'll never go as fast as your alpine friends.
- You'll fall more often.
- It's rare to catch big air on tele-gear.
- Your legs will get worked.
- Telemark skiing is amazingly beautiful!

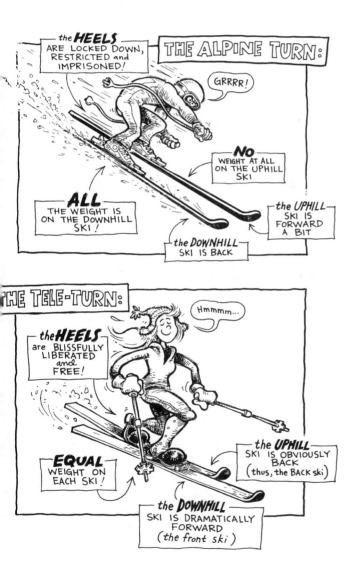

4 The gear (quick and dirty)

A friend showed up at my door the other day all excited about the great deal he just got on a pair of skis. However, when he showed me what he'd bought, all I could do was shake my head in sadness—too skinny, too long, and too stiff. While these skis might have been used for telemarking at one time (back in the days when dinosaurs roamed the earth), they would only prolong his misery when he was learning to turn. Those skis would be fine for touring across golf courses in Minnesota, but if you want to turn, then get skis that turn. Stay away from gear that "does it all." If you are new to telemark skiing and want to ski downhill (making telemark turns!), then start off with the right type of equipment.

Skis: Nowadays there are millions of good tele-skis on the market. If you are getting new skis then you probably don't need to worry as long as the store in your town sells telemark gear and you haven't maxed out your credit card. If, on the other hand,

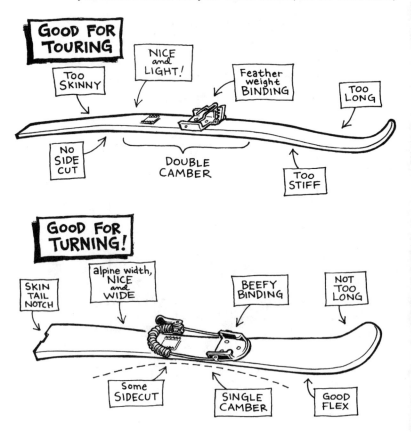

your pocketbook dictates you shop at the nearest thrift store, look for boards that are wide. An old pair of alpine boards mounted with free-heel bindings are a great (and cheap) way to start out in the sport. Don't worry about high-performance skis; these can wait until you're ready for high-performance turns. For now, old alpine skis will turn just fine.

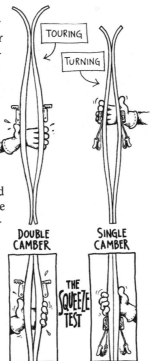

Skis that are skinny and stiff and have a groove down the middle are made for touring, not downhill per-formance. In fact, these skis are almost impossible to turn. Tour-ing skis are double-cambered and have a wax pocket. When squeezed together in the middle, a gap will exist between the bases under the foot. Tele-skis are single camber and are easy to squeeze together.

good for TURNING

TALL, STIFF and HEAVY DUTY!

Boots: Same deal as skis. If you are getting used boots then get ones designed for going downhill versus "cross country". The cuff should at least come up over your ankle, and the sole should be stiff like a pair of heavy-duty hiking boots.

good for TOURING

LIGHT, LOW and COMFY

5 The fall line

This is the same line a beach ball will take if it is rolled down a hill. The ball only wants to go one way: It wants to follow the path of least resistance and the pull of gravity. This is what skiing is all about—embracing gravity. You want to ski in the fall line. Turns are used to check your speed and provide you with a sense of control. It is especially important to always have your upper body facing down the fall line. This makes for quicker turns because you only have to maneuver half your body (the lower half) across and through the fall line. It also helps you keep your weight over your skis (as opposed to your rear end).

BACK
foot is up on
it's toes,
way too high
in
the heel!

FRONT
foot's ankle ain't
bent, it's at a
90° angle

LOUSY STANCE!

BACK
foot is balanced
on the
BALL of the foot
and
the heel is LOW!

FRONT
foot's ankle is
bent forward

FABULOUS STANCE!

6 The stance

A good telemark position begins with the "stance." Where your feet are and how you stand on 'em is the heart and soul of the telemark position. A basic stance for many activities is called the athletic stance. This is a nice, stable body position that involves keeping your knees bent, your shoulders low, and your hands out in front of your body. Think of a soccer goalie getting ready to block a penalty kick; this is what you want to aim for. You want to be both loose and ready to spring into action (see Tip 73). From this position you can now drop into the tele-stance.

Let's start with the downhill foot, also known as the outside or front foot. Your knee should be directly above the toes of your front foot. Both the ankle and knee should be bent, giving you a forward cant. Your front boot will be hidden from view by your knee when you are in a good tele-position.

Now the uphill foot, also known as the inside or back foot. This foot is bent at the toe with the heel lifted off the back ski. You support half your weight on this foot, so stand on the ball of the foot and not on your tippy-toes. Try and keep that heel as low as you can, but still off the ski. Both knees should be snugged up close. Your thighs should be at an angle pointing down toward the snow. You should feel the same loose-but-ready-to-go attitude as you did in the athletic stance.

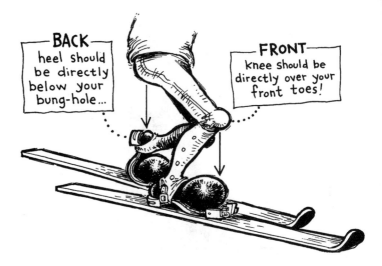

BACK — heel should be directly below your bung-hole...

FRONT — knee should be directly over your front toes!

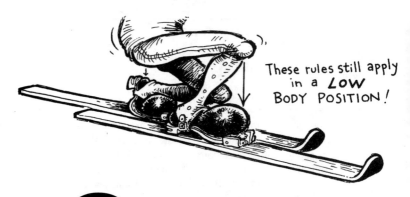

These rules still apply in a *LOW* BODY POSITION!

⑦ Be above your skis

The position of your body is very important for a good stance. You always want to be directly above your skis, because it's your body weight that controls them. If they get out from under you, there's no way to weight 'em. The front foot is rarely a problem because you're steering with it. It's that pesky back foot that seems to demand a lot of attention. Ignore it, and it starts to trail along behind you. It's very important to keep that back foot directly under you. Your heel needs to be exactly under your butt. If your calf muscle is targeted below your butt instead, that back foot is too far back. Whether your stance is high or low, these rules don't change. If you get low, stay compact so the weight stays above your skis. If you make the mistake of getting too spread out you'll lose control of your skis.

8 Falling down

It goes without saying that the goal is to avoid falling down. However, the reality is that it's inevitable and unavoidable. Besides, there are advantages to falling down—it's a sure-fire way to stop—so therefore it is worth knowing how to do it right, so that you can avoid going BOOM and maybe blowing out a knee. Being able to stop instantly is a very important thing to know when

you find yourself out of control or when that tree jumps out of nowhere into your path. Another advantage to falling down is that it doesn't take a lot of practice, so you can feel successful right away.

The best way to fall down is to fall off to one side (usually uphill) and land on your butt, since that's where most of the padding is. To get up again, position your skis underneath you and across the fall line; then push your weight up over the top of them. In deep powder it helps to lay your poles on the snow and push off of them.

MELLOW SLOPE

tele-position

Rise up!

Sink back down into the TELE-POSITION

9 The tele-shuffle

This is the most basic tip in the book. This simple exercise helps reinforce the telemark stance. It should be practiced until you have it ingrained in your memory. Find a mellow slope (no need to bring fear into the equation) and ski slowly across it. As you ski across, gently drop into the tele-position. Think about sinking down from a nice athletic stance into your tele-stance, downhill foot forward. Next, gently rise up to an athletic stance and sink back down again into that same tele-position. Practice rising up and sinking back down in both directions across the slope. You want to get comfortable gliding while you switch back and forth between stances.

just like
WALKING

tele-position

Rise up
and
TRANSITION!

Sink back down
into
OPPOSITE
TELE-POSITION!

⑩ Transition

Once you master the previous tip, you're ready for the transition. Cross the same slope you were on before, but now switch the lead foot each time you drop back down into the tele-position. Think extension as you rise up and compression as you sink down. Find a rhythm, same as if you were walking. Don't pause in between steps—each step should just flow from the one before. But unlike walking, there is an equal push and pull in the movement of the skis. This is called the straight-run telemark, and the up and down motion is at the heart of a lot of the advanced tips in this book. So get into this good habit early.

11 The turn

Once again, let's start by crossing that same mellow slope. As you begin to ski across the slope, initiate your turn by dropping into a tele-position with your uphill (outside) leg in front. Point your upper body downhill and rotate your knees and ankles in the direction you want to go. Think compression and your skis should arch around as you turn. This turning action lets you dump some speed as well. The turn finishes with your outside (now it's downhill) ski still in front and all you have to do is rise up, transition, and start over again.

12 The patience turn

If you are having trouble getting the feel for the transition or you're experiencing problems getting into the fall line, this exercise will help. This is also an easy way to begin linking turns together. Do this drill on a mellow slope and let the fall line do the work.

Start with a gentle traverse, simply allowing the skis to seek the fall line. Do nothing; just relax and let those skis naturally make a gentle turn in the direction of gravity. Wait until you are pointing downhill, then sink down into the turn and compress and edge those skis out of the fall line. When you complete the turn by coming across the fall line, simply stand back up in your athletic stance, and let the skis start back into the fall line. As you get more comfortable with this, you can transition faster and edge your skis into the fall line just like in the previous tip.

the FALL line

12

13 Tele-circle

This is another good drill to practice. Pick a comfortable slope for yourself and get into a tele-stance with your downhill (inside) leg back, and the uphill (outside) leg forward (just like it would be if you were initiating a turn). This starting point is the top of a circle, 12 o'clock. The idea here is to scribe a circle with your skis. As you start down, keep your upper body facing down the fall line, and point your knees and ankles in the direction of the circle. You should ride smoothly through the fall line and across it, coming to stop somewhere around 4 o'clock. Finish the circle by herring boning back up the slope to 12 o'clock, and start all over again. Do this multiple times, smoothing it all out, so that each circle flows into the next one. Then switch directions and work on your turn going the other way. Have someone stand at the bottom of the circle and review your technique. Remember to keep your body facing downhill throughout the turn.

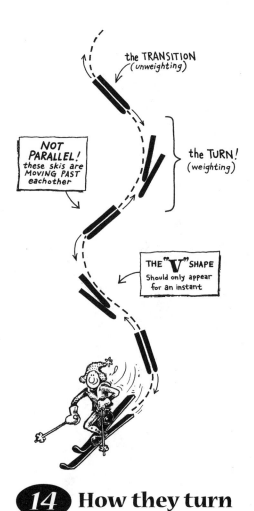

the TRANSITION
(unweighting)

NOT PARALLEL!
these skis are
MOVING PAST
eachother

the TURN!
(weighting)

THE "V" SHAPE
Should only appear
for an instant

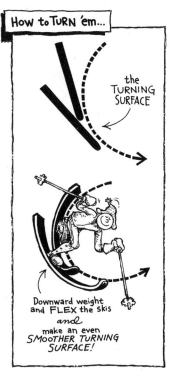

How to TURN 'em...

the TURNING SURFACE

Downward weight
and FLEX the skis
and
make an even
SMOOTHER TURNING
SURFACE!

14 How they turn

When two skis are in the telemark position they create a delicate "V" pattern. This "V" shape is what early skiers relied on to help them turn. In those early days of pure wooden skis, nobody thought to shape the ski with a tip and tail that were wider than the waist of the ski (today this is known as sidecut). Early telemarkers compensated for this lack of sidecut by slightly off-setting the skis while making turns (this is the "V" pâttern). This "V" pattern created a natural sidecut and helped turn the ski. While not entirely necessary with today's sidecut skis, this "V" shape is still an integral part of the tele-turn and is one of the things that make it so beautiful. Watch any good skier on easy terrain as they make nice, rounded turns, and you will see the skis melt in and out of each turn with a subtle "V" shape.

15 Keep your skis snugged together

The subtle "V" shape that shows up in mid-telemark turn has its limitations, however. The problem is that sometimes it isn't so subtle and then it can become a problem. Often the beginning telemarker will allow the uphill ski to get into an overly obtuse angle, and the "V" gets way too big. Then the back ski turns into an outrigger that works against the turn. What you want is to have both skis snugged together nice and close. A good skier can snap back-and-forth between turns without any "V" shape at all. But most skiers will let a little of this angle creep into their skiing style, if only for a nano-second at the sharpest point of their turn.

16 Crossing the fall line

  If you actually pointed your skis straight down the fall line and let gravity take over, you could easily reach mach speeds (even on the bunny slope) that you may find to be a bit intimidating. Turns provide us with maneuverability, and by making turns back and forth across the fall line we can control our speed. When we turn our skis across the slope, though, it's important to keep our upper body in the fall line. This helps maximize what we can do with our skis.

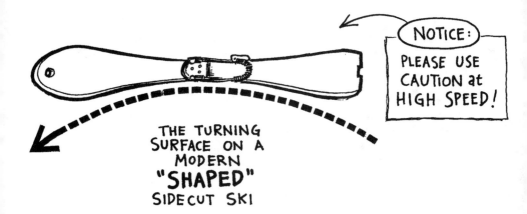

THE TURNING
SURFACE ON A
MODERN
"SHAPED"
SIDECUT SKI

NOTICE:
PLEASE USE
CAUTION at
HIGH SPEED!

17 Sidecut

Your skis are equipped with some degree of sidecut, which means they're wider at the tip and tail and thinner at the waist. Some skis have a little sidecut, while others, such as the modern "shaped" skis (parabolic) have a really dramatic sidecut. This newer design really gets those skis to turn, and they are amazingly responsive (and fun!) to use. In fact, it's hard not to turn with these skis. The parabolic sidecut—used in combination with a tall stance, dramatic weighting, and camber reversal—can make for some amazingly quick turns with relatively little effort.

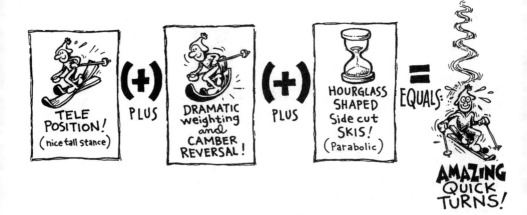

TELE POSITION! (nice tall stance) **PLUS (+)** DRAMATIC weighting and CAMBER REVERSAL! **PLUS (+)** HOURGLASS SHAPED Side cut SKIS! (Parabolic) **EQUALS =** AMAZING QUICK TURNS!

18 Sit on your heels

If you are having trouble getting the feel for the tele-stance, or if your back leg seems to be trailing behind like a neighbor's dog instead of helping you turn, try "sitting on your heel." Sitting on your heel forces you to put weight on that back ski and you'll get a feel for where that ski belongs. This exercise also helps center you over the skis. You'll also build up those thigh muscles when you switch lead skis back and forth.

19 Knee to the ski

Yet another tip to help you get the feel for the tele-stance. Try touching your knee to the ski as you drop into a telemark. This will help center you over your skis. It's a good idea to wear knee pads for this one.

20 Tuck your knee in

This tip has two parts: The first part will help you get the feel for the tele-position and where your stance should be; the second part is for those skiers who are trying to tighten up their stance.

With your knee pads off, carefully fit the knee cap of your back leg into the hollow spot behind the knee of your front leg. This trick will keep you from standing too tall or getting too low in your stance. Practice some tele-shuffles using this technique.

This trick also works wonders if you're trying to tighten up your stance. Think about tucking the knee of your back leg behind the knee of your front leg during each turn. This keeps your knees close together and under your body, which is what you want.

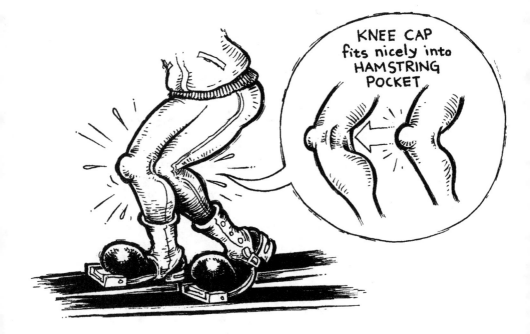

KNEE CAP fits nicely into HAMSTRING POCKET

21 Touch the snow

This simple drill works great to get your body facing downhill. Allow yourself to sink into a nice low position; then, with your uphill hand, reach down and touch the snow on the downhill side of your skis. You can hold that finger

UPHILL FINGER
reaching across to the
DOWNHILL SNOW
makes a great
body position!

there and scribe a line while you do a long traverse. (If you're new to telemarking and this feels like too much, practice first by using your downhill hand instead of your uphill hand. The position this creates isn't ideal, but it's a good introduction.) Try this drill in combo with Tip 18 (Sit on your heels) and Tip 19 (Knee to the ski) after you have mastered them. Or try alternating those finger taps with each turn.

22 Feel the tongue

If you are getting the front leg of your tele-position correct, you will feel pressure on the front of your shin from the tongue of your boot. You definitely don't want to feel the opposite (pressure on the back of your calf). The only way to feel the pressure from your tongue is to bend forward at the ankle.

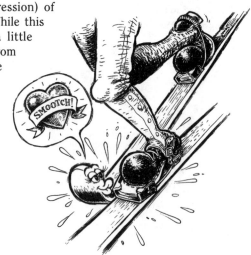

23 Let your tip kiss your binding

In the beginning, when you're working on getting that feel for the tele-position, think of letting your ski tip "kiss" the binding of the other ski at the low point (compression) of each turn. While this position is a little spread out from what you're eventually shooting for, it's a nice visual way for you to work on your stance.

24 Airplane wings

This is a great mental and visual exercise that helps beginners smooth out the herky-jerky motions of the upper body. Imagine yourself with airplane wings carefully balanced on your shoulders. The key to a safe flight is to keep your aircraft pointed down the hill. Your legs will be doing all the work, so try and keep your upper body quiet and smooth. The airplane should move gracefully down the slope, gently banking, and riding up and down as you weight (compress) and unweight (extend) your skis.

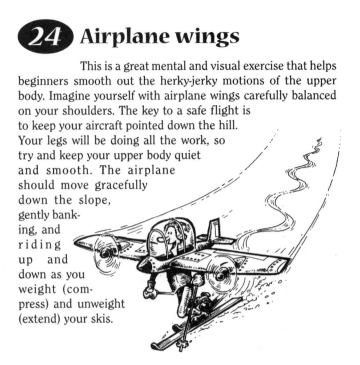

25 Toy train tracks

Do you freeze between turns, holding your compressed telemark position for a long traverse before you get the gumption to extend and turn again? If so, the solution is easy.

Imagine you are riding on a toy train track. The track is made up of straight sections and curved sections. The novice skier will hold a long traverse on the straight tracks before committing to each turn. The advanced skier, however, uses only the curves, simply rising and sinking into each turn as if no straight track exists at all—each turn flows directly from the one before it. If you get frozen into position, all you need to do is remove the straight track and only ski the curves.

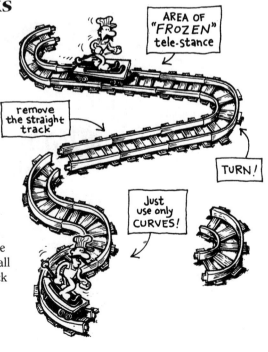

AREA OF "FROZEN" tele-stance

remove the straight track

TURN!

Just use only CURVES!

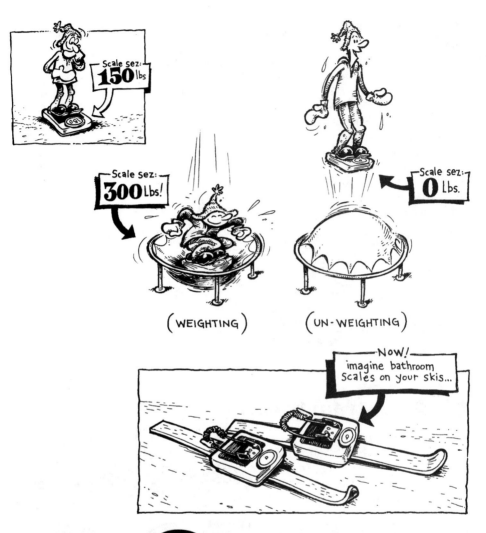

(WEIGHTING)   (UN-WEIGHTING)

Now!
imagine bathroom
scales on your skis...

26 The concept of weighting and unweighting

Skiing is not a standstill, static endeavor. Rather, it's a dynamic sport with lots of motion beyond just the glisse of your skis. There are some wonderful laws of physics that you can use to your advantage.

Our little skier is shown here on a bathroom scale, weighing-in at a fit 150 pounds. As long as he is standing still, the scale will continue to show his weight as 150 lbs. Now suppose we were to glue that scale to his feet and get him bouncing on a trampoline.

At his lowest point (in compression) that scale reads 300 lbs., or double his standing weight. That weighting creates some powerful energy in the trampoline (or in your skis). In the next instant he is shot up (extension), and for one moment, at the highest point in his ride, he is weightless—the scale registers zero. So in a blink of an eye our skier goes from doubling his weight to zero-gravity. This concept of weighting and unweighting is a fundamental of skiing. Lets see what happens when we put these scales on our skis.

27 Weighting and unweighting

The essential secret to maneuvering your skis back and forth across the fall line is the ability to weight and unweight your skis. By weighting your skis you push the camber out of them, and even reverse it. This causes the skis to bow under your feet and this shape lends itself to a turn. When you unweight the ski you are in a sense lifting it up off the snow. In this instant of zero-gravity, it's easy to change the direction of the ski, switch leads, and shift your balance to the other set of edges. Then as you weight the ski again you force it into the next turn.

the Transition
(UN- WEIGHTING)
Extension

So how do you accomplish this incredible feat? Basically by doing knee bends. When you bend your knees, the weight of your body begins to move in a downward motion (compression). It's this transfer of momentum to the skis which "weights" them and causes them to bend underneath you. As you reverse this by standing up again (extension), your momentum takes an upward trajectory and 'unweights' the skis.

the TURN!
(WEIGHTING)
Compression

Another way to think of this is as a coiled spring. As you compress (get shorter by bending the knees) the spring pushes down on the skis, weighting them. Then as you spring up, the skis no longer have that weight pushing down on them, and they jump back to their original shape, waiting for you to redirect them.

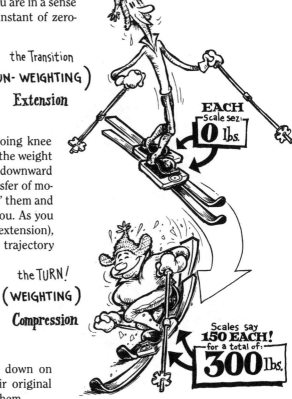

EACH
Scale sez:
0 lbs.

Scales say
150 EACH!
for a total of:
300 lbs.

28 Equal weighting

Look at our perfect tele-skier as he gently rides 'em: The scales for his front and back feet each read exactly 75 pounds. Each foot is balancing half his body weight. (If he were working on his compression, these scales would total more than his body weight, so let's pretend he's just holding a nice long arcing turn.) This skill of equal weighting will do more to make you a perfect tele-skier than any other tip in this book.

Now look at our lame skier: He's only weighting his front ski while completely ignoring his back ski. He's setting himself up for disaster because it simply won't work this way. On a hard-packed surface such as a ski area or corn snow, it's natural to weight the front ski more than the back. This helps the ski bite (or more correctly, edge) into the snow. And since you are supposed to be facing down the fall line, there is a more natural sense of balance. However, this can lead to problems. If you don't get enough weight on the back ski, it assumes you don't care for it and subsequently it goes wherever it wants. This lack of control makes the back ski squirrelly, and often leads to the unwanted scenario of crossed skis. Concentrate on really weighting that back ski. As you do a turn, feel yourself push down on that ski and push it through the turn. You might be able to cheat a little on the groomers, but on a powder day, it's incredibly important to have your weight evenly distributed over both skis. This creates a platform for you to ride on. In powder the most frequent cause of head plants is putting too much weight on the front ski. This causes it to dive into the snow and stop—while the momentum of your upper body throws you forward into a face plant.

29 Use the ski's rebound

Set your skis flat on the ground and look at them. They should touch the floor at the tip and tail and rise up to a high point somewhere under the binding. (If they don't do this then it's time to get a new pair.) The fact that your skis do this is all part of the grand design and is known as camber. Now push down in the middle of them until they are perfectly flat on the floor....and then let go. What did they do? They snapped back up. We use this rebounding quality to help us turn our skis.

On the slopes, as the skier unweights, the skis spring up as well, helping to create a weightless moment for the transition into the next turn. The skier then weights the skis again, forcing them to scribe an arch.

30 Slide the back foot forward

As you end one turn, slide that rear foot forward into the next.
Think about putting pressure on it as you move it forward.
This will help you weight your back ski and make for a nice,
smooth transition into the next turn. The tele-turn is a series of
beautiful flowing motions, and your focus should be on moving
forward. This is a nice, positive mental image for the beginner to
focus on while on gentle terrain. For a smoother transition think
back foot slides forward.

31 Slide the front foot back

Now let's contradict the previous tip. There are times when you want to flip the previous mindset around. When skiing the steeps or a bump run you want to snap through each transition really quick. That front ski needs to slide quickly backward to its stable position under you. In reality you should be pushing and pulling equally on each ski in the transition. It's the focus of your mental energy that changes. For a faster transition think front ski slides back.

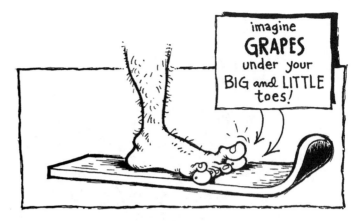

32 Big toe, little toe

This is a sure-fire way to make you focus on your edging. Pretend you have grapes positioned under your big and little toes. When you are doing a turn, you want to squish the grape under your big toe with your downhill foot. With your uphill foot, you squish the grape under your little toe. Be aggressive with this grape flattening pressure, because it's this action, from your toe to your ski, that makes those edges bite into the snow. A glass of wine (squeezed from your socks) after skiing is a good way to celebrate your success.

BIG TOE, LITTLE TOE transfers directly to the uphill EDGES!

33 Legs as springs

There are two reasons for you to think of your bottom half as a spring. First, your legs are what you use to absorb those irregularities that occur in the snowpack. With free heel bindings, the tele-position is really one of the best things going for absorbing a bump or inconsistency in the snow, because it provides both front and back stability. So as you bash through lumpy snow, let the spring do all the work and keep a quiet upper body. The legs are your shock absorbers.

Second, imagine springing out of the end of each turn and then compressing down at the start of the next. That feeling of springing up and then dropping into the next turn is where much of the fun in skiing lies.

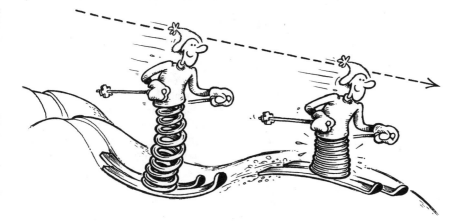

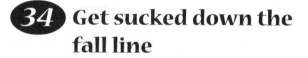

THE FALL LINE

VVRRRR!

34 Get sucked down the fall line

Imagine you have a long piece of string protruding from your belly button. The other end is stuck in a giant vacuum cleaner down slope, exactly in line with the fall line. The instant you push off for your run, the vacuum gets turned on. You get sucked down the fall line. That string (gravity) wants to pull you down the hill. Don't fight it! If you get out of the fall line or hold a turn too long, that string will get stressed out and torque you off balance. Don't let that happen—embrace gravity and ski the fall line.

THE
FALL
LINE!

35 A flashlight in your belly button

As you ski down the hill, you want to keep your upper body facing down the fall line. Think of your belly button as a flashlight that you must keep pointed directly down the hill. This mental image works because it forces you to point your hips down the fall line.

By rotating your hips you can DIRECT the Beam!

36 Use short poles

You want those hands in front of you, not above your head somewhere. If you are making your turns from a low stance, you want short poles. This makes it easier to keep your hands in front of you. Skiing with long poles is great as long as you have a nice tall stance. But long poles and a short stance don't work; you end up in that classic "Praise the Lord" pose. Shorten your adjustable-probe poles, or steal a pair from a five year old.

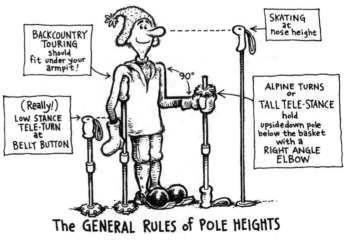

The GENERAL RULES of POLE HEIGHTS

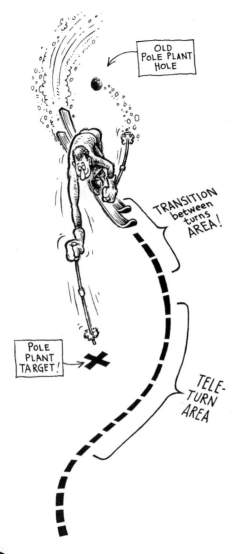

(37) Reach downhill

Reaching aggressively downhill with each pole plant has many benefits. For one thing, it sets your body up for the next turn because it keeps your upper body in the fall line. This puts you in a great position to make quick turns using just your lower body. Second, reaching downhill keeps you leaning downhill. It doesn't allow your body to lean uphill into the slope. By concentrating on downhill pole plants, you can break the bad habit of uphill pole plants. Third, reaching aggressively downhill helps keep both hands out in front of you, which is exactly what you want.

the BASKET comes around in sync with the turn

REACH!

NEXT POLE PLANT TARGET!

38 Timing downhill pole plants

To keep you in the fall line, you need to make your pole plants downhill. Timing is crucial. You plant your pole downhill of yourself when you're at the lowest point of your compression. This initiates the next turn. As you rise up out of your turn, you should already be thinking about the next pole plant and reaching for it. The hand that just planted the pole should be swinging back across your body, to point down the fall line. You don't want to let it get behind you. Keep your hands where you can see them at all times.

SINK DOWN
into
POLE PLANT

Just
quickly
"STING"
the snow

39 Turn around the pole plant

After you plant your pole, ski around it and set up for the next pole plant. Don't let your pole linger in the snow—just sting the slope with it, and as you ski around it, snap it out. You should already be thinking about the next pole plant and reaching downhill for it. Don't lean on a pole after it's planted; it's not there for support, it's just a tool for timing. Also, your uphill hand (or shoulder) shouldn't linger anywhere behind you. Keep reaching forward.

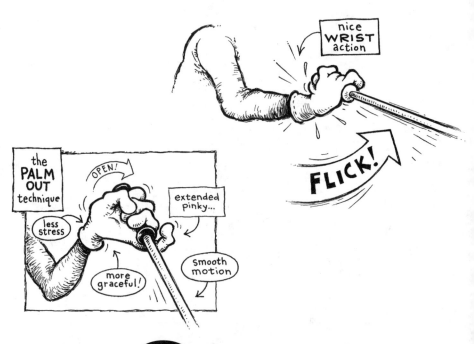

40 Use your wrist

For a nice quick pole plant, flick the pole out in front of you with your wrist. You can also think about keeping your palm facing out. This will help open your body up to the fall line, and it actually gives you more reach with each pole plant. Imagine opening a curtain with your downhill hand with each turn.

41 Punch downhill with that uphill hand

This is a good aggressive way to get your uphill hand back in front of you after each pole plant. Just imagine socking some-one shorter than you down the fall line. Don't hold back, you can forcefully lead with your shoulder to get some KO power. Also, having your hands down the hill keeps you from leaning into the slope behind you. It keeps your mass moving down-ward and not back into the slope, which would cause you to skid out.

Also, when you let your hands lag behind you after a turn, you aren't set up for your next turn. Keeping those hands out in front assures that your upper body is rotated down the fall line and in a good balanced position. You'll be ready for your next pole plant.

42 Know the pros and cons of getting low and standing tall

There is no right or wrong here, it's all skiing and you can make beautiful turns either way. Both these skiers are in the exact same point in their turn, but one is demonstrating the low style while the other is "standing tall." Each of these styles has its place and its pros and cons. A versatile skier will be strong in both positions as there are places and snow conditions that favor each one.

Getting Low (old school style)

- very stable
- short poles help
- lotta work on a long day
- if you fall, you're closer to the snow
- knees are more exposed in a fall
- easier to get face shots
- looks cool
- performs well in crud and on the steeps

Standing Tall (the modern look)

- quicker and easier transition from turn to turn
- plastic boots favor this stance
- hard to ski under low branches.
- higher center of gravity
- easier on the knees
- more spring in your legs to absorb bumps
- performs well on groomers, corn and powder

NICE STRONG "C" STANCE!

43 The "C" stance

By facing down the hill and reaching for it with your upper body, you create more torque to help bring your skis around. You should feel your body make a "C." This arcing shape begins with your toes and follows right up through your head. If you stand upright (like the letter "I"), it becomes harder to twist your hips so they face downhill. The steeper the slope, the greater "C" stance you want. (It is not necessary to arch much on a low angle slope.)

Avoid the "I" STANCE!

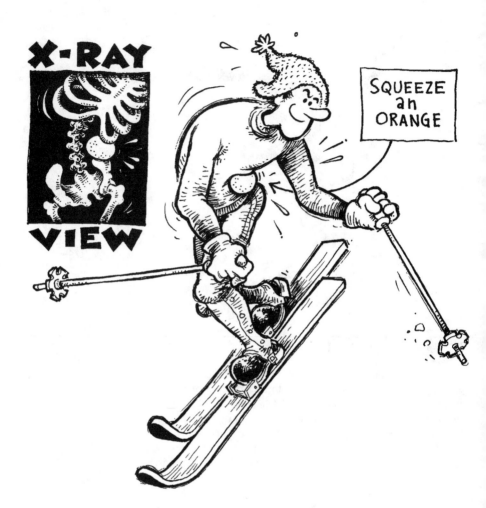

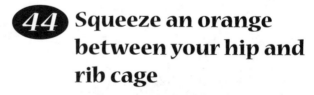

44 Squeeze an orange between your hip and rib cage

You can get a good feel for the arcing "C" stance by thinking about squeezing an orange between your hip and ribs. As you alternate between each turn, think about gripping that orange. This creates a dramatic curve in your body.

PRETTY GOOD STANCE...

BEND FORWARD

AWESOME STANCE!

45 Bend at that hip

You can squeeze more power out of your "C" stance by aggressively bending forward from the hip. This extra forward lean creates a powerful body position that brings those skis around with more snap. It also keeps you weighted over your skis (which helps them hold on the snow vs. slipping out from underneath you). It should feel like your upper body is gracefully falling down the hill as you make each turn. Bending at the hip allows your upper body to lead the way.

46 Lead with your chin

When you lean your body downhill, don't lead with your nose—that forces you to look at your ski tips. Lead with your chin—that forces you to look downhill. If you put your chin out in front, it actually lines your body up in a strong and powerful stance. It really works! With poor chin technique, every part of your body position suffers.

(skidding)

the
STRAIGHT
"I"
STANCE

CH-CHA-
CHATTER!

47 Carving vs. skidding

The previous tips, besides helping you turn your skis
quicker, will also help you carve your turns on the hardpack. If
your skis are skidding out from underneath you or chattering on
the snow, then you need to get more weight over them. Keeping
your upper-body weight over your skis makes them hold well
through your turn. So use an aggressive "C" stance and bend at
your hip to keep you over your skis. Thinking about making
downhill pole plants will also help you achieve this.

48 Practice the body position

This simple exercise helps you recognize (and feel) the proper body position for tele-turns. Have a friend stand below you in the fall line. Hand her (or him) your poles and make her lean back and pull (a big friend works great in this role). Maintain the tele-position across the fall line, and fight that pull. You need to work against the downhill tugging, and when you do, you'll score a bunch of excellent style points. It's a natural instinct to set yourself up in an amazing and perfect telemark stance. Focus on this in each direction, and work on creating some muscle memory that will help you turn.

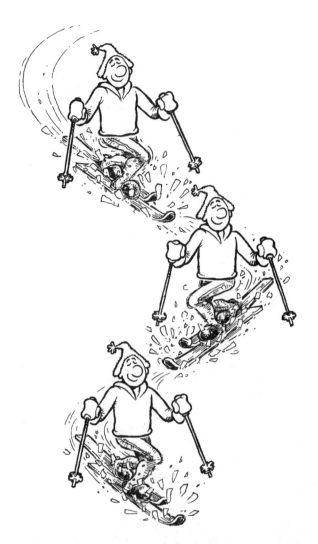

49 Quiet upper body

Ever watch those gnarly ski videos of rad dudes skiing impossibly steep snow fields? Take note of their upper bodies (from the waist up). You will notice that while their skis are turning this way and that, their upper torso is relatively quiet. It stays facing down the fall line without a lot of twisting back and forth. It is this independent motion that allows a graceful transition from one turn to the next. The upper body is anticipating each turn as the legs go through the motions of the turn.

PARALLEL

UPHILL HIP

UPHILL SKI IS OUT FRONT

SOGGY dishrag DEMO

Only a slight twist to the body is required

TELEMARK

UPHILL HIP

UPHILL SKI IS BACK

You need to dramatically twist and lunge to properly face downhill!

𝟓𝟎 Parallel vs. tele-twist

This book talks a lot about twisting your upper body so you face downhill. Our parallel turning brothers (and sisters) need to twist too, but not as much as we do. The reason is the different positions of our uphill skis. The parallel skier has the uphill ski forward; this transfers to the uphill hip, causing it to face down the fall line with minimal twisting. This is an advantage to the parallel turn.

In the telemark turn, the uphill ski is back. This opens the hip up to the hill, but you want to keep that hip facing down the fall line. You need to dramatically twist and lunge to properly face downhill. No matter how you ski—using parallel or telemark turns—you always want to have those hips facing downhill.

51 Breathe

This may sound ridiculous, but when your mind is swamped with a dozen little tricks to remember, you can actually forget to breathe. This has some obvious detrimental effects, like oxygen debt. It's very hard to link a bunch of turns together if your muscles are oxygen starved. You also look a little silly bent over your poles halfway down the slope, gasping for air as everyone else zooms by. If you are forgetting to breathe, then tell yourself to take a breath with each turn. Don't be afraid to huff and puff out loud. Besides being good practice for natural child birth, it will help you get into a rhythm.

52 Stay relaxed

When you get all tensed up, your muscles stiffen up and no longer perform. You simply can't rotate, reach down the hill, or unweight your skis. In a relaxed state, your muscles are ready to spring into action and do what their muscle memory (and hopefully your brain) want. Good skiers make it look easy because their turns are free of tension. It's easy to spot someone who is relaxed when skiing.

53 Enjoy the skin back up

Even though you don't see many pictures in magazines featuring the skin track, it's still a part of skiing. And if you want to ski away from the lifts, it's a necessity. So enjoy the skin track, it's part of your work out, it's out in the beautiful mountains (versus behind a desk), and your lungs are filled with clean air. If the backcountry is a new experience, don't get frustrated because you have to hike uphill, there are plenty of benefits to earning your turns. God gave you your own high-speed "quads," so enjoy using them.

54 Before your run

Don't just peel 'em and squeal 'em! When you are skinning (or booting) uphill in the backcountry, take a few minutes to collect yourself after that long hump up. You've earned it. Do all the important things before your run to insure success. Enjoy the view, drink some water, center your karma and pick out that perfect line...then let 'er rip.

Just one
m-m-more
run...

55 Know when to call it a day

If you're skiing lousy at the end of a long day, don't add exhaustion to your problems. Go home (and study this book!) before you need to call a knee surgeon.

56 Get used to skiing with a pack

When you ski in the backcountry you need to carry a pack with a few essentials. If you've never skied with a pack, don't complain when you cut those first few turns with extra poundage on your back. It gets to be second nature pretty quickly after you put some time in. You can make life a little easier by not overpacking. In fact, there's a really cool book mentioned soon hereafter that gives great info on what you need to carry.

Sometimes it's nice to leave your pack at the top of your run. But even then you need to carry a minimum amount of gear, such as an avalanche beacon and shovel.

57 Get Allen and Mike's other book!

The skills needed for backcountry skiing go way beyond the humble telemark turn. We worked hard to fill *Allen and Mike's Really Cool Backcountry Ski Book* with all the info you'd ever need for camping and traveling in the winter. Maybe this tip seems like shameless self-promotion (it is), but these two books are designed to complement each other. Part of the joy of tele-skis is the fact you can use them in the backcountry. We know you will be better prepared with these books on your shelf, or better yet...in your backpack!

58 Find a mantra

"Relax and breathe." This is a good mantra and it really works! Say it before you push off downhill and repeat it with each turn. The advantage of a mantra is that it helps set a rhythm for nice, even turns. "Unweight, bounce, quick turns, embrace gravity," or "face downhill"– these are all good mantras. Thinking about your pole plants can help. Whatever you use, keep it simple and pick one thing to focus on for each run. Don't swamp your mind with every tip in the book. If you do that, nothing will work. A little positive energy goes a long way, so visualize success.

59 Keep the parallel turn in your bag of tricks

Parallel turns in a telemark book? Well, if you already know how to ski in an alpine stance, don't assume you will never use this turn on free-heel skis. It's totally worth knowing how to telemark and parallel, because the two turns will complement each other. If you have a lifetime of alpine skiing and the tele-turn is a new thing for you, the parallel turn is a great position to fall back on when things get out of hand.

(TURN)   (TURN)

(Transition)

➏⓿ Use your tassel to counterbalance your knees

The pivotal counter balance technique is often ignored by the closed-minded scientific community. Surprisingly, the collective mass and velocity of the hat tassel can be used to create a powerful leveling energy center. The transition (and alternation) of this rhythmic gravity output results in a new and amazing skill/ dynamism.

Hat in the easy position

61 Squeeze an orange between your legs

One common problem among people learning to telemark is that they get too spread out. Although a wide stance and high hands is the classic old picture of tele-skiers, a tight stance is what you should shoot for in this day and age of advanced equipment and technique. Keeping your feet and legs close together allows for a faster transition between turns. Also, a tighter stance will give you more stability and an increased ability to absorb irregularities in the snow.

So develop a tight stance. As an exercise, try holding a hat, scarf, pole, glove, or whatever between your legs as you link turns. Skiing with an orange between your legs is especially tricky, because it's round and slippery against nylon pants. After practicing a while with the real thing, all you will need to do is imagine holding something be-

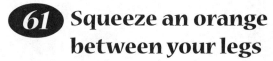

an Orange in the technically ADVANCED position!

tween your legs. This exercise forces you to keep your legs together as you ski.

62 Use a lurk

If you were skiing a hundred years ago in the snowy countryside of Norway, you'd certainly be holding your trusty lurk. What's a lurk? It's a long wooden staff. Early in this century someone got the idea of using two poles (holding one in each hand). However, the single-pole technique of yore has some advantages when you're learning to turn, because you hold it with both hands. This forces you to fully rotate and keep your hands out in front of you, which in turn keeps your weight over your skis. Try this exercise: Hold your lurk out in front of you like a kayak paddle and try to tap the snow with the end on the downhill side. Actually, you may choose to drag the tip, but that's good form too. Instead of mail-ordering a real lurk from Norway, simply try extending your probe poles out to a nice long length.

63 Focus on something downhill

When you drive down the highway, are your focused on the pavement directly below your grill? No! You want to drink in the big picture and focus on that vanishing point up ahead. Same with skiing. Pick something down slope to focus on. It can be anything: a tree, a lump of snow or your partner. Make sure it is directly down the fall line and ski toward it. Keep more than your eyes on it—focus your entire upper body on it. Think about hugging it. Of course it's advised that you stop or pick another object to focus on once you get close. Otherwise you might ski into it.

64 Do a run with loose boots

Dare yourself to do this. You need to perfectly center yourself over your skis. No cheating allowed. This demands that you find the sweet spot over your skis. This is where you want to be skiing. You might never find this delicate point of balance with your boots cranked down tight.

(65) Spoon the tracks of a better skier

This is an especially good tip if you are trying to figure out how to make those same nice tracks. It helps push you to learn a new style of skiing and make a cleaner line. It may help you develop that rhythm you have been missing. Plus you'll sleep better at night knowing you use this guilt-free technique of eco-groovy powder conservation.

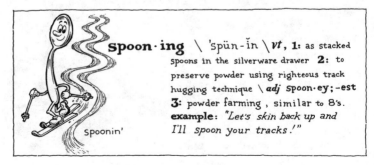

spoon·ing \ 'spün-in \ *vt*, **1:** as stacked spoons in the silverware drawer **2:** to preserve powder using righteous track hugging technique \ *adj* spoon·ey;-est **3:** powder farming , similar to 8's. **example:** *"Let's skin back up and I'll spoon your tracks!"*

Spoonin'

66 Ski without your poles

Going without your poles helps improve your balance and gives you one less thing to think about. Concentrate on facing down the hill with your upper body. Too many skiers depend on their poles as an extra point of balance. This exercise is a real eye opener because you are unable to cheat. You are forced into a balanced stance. Pretend you are delivering a tray of fine wine to your friends down the fall line.

67 Rooster-tail off the back ski

This is a great way to get you shifting more weight to that back ski. While difficult to do, it's easy to imagine. Concentrate on throwing all your weight and power on your back ski. As a mental exercise, this can help you break the habit of too much weight on the front ski.

68 Review your tracks

Skiing gracefully is an expressive art form. The tracks you create are really works of art that can tell you a lot about your skiing. Here's what to look for:

- Are the pole plants on the inside of the turns? (Downhill pole plants should be.)
- Are the turns even? (If you have a "bad" side, those turns are usually bigger.)
- Are you hesitating somewhere in your turn? (This will be evidenced by a traversing track.)
- Are the transitions smooth? (If they're too fast, they'll look "Z" shaped.)
- Are the tracks too straight? (Round them out and finish each turn.)

the track is
nice and
SNAPPY!

69 Make short fast turns

If you feel stuck in long wide turns, this tip may be all you need. Simply making quicker turns might be what it takes to bring it all together. On an easy slope, work on quick transitions between turns. Make each one short and fast. The moment you start to turn out of the fall line, unweight and make the transition into the next turn. Think about weighting and unweighting your skis aggressively. Being able to do short radius turns is a good thing to have in your bag of tricks for certain snow conditions and for skiing in the trees.

Ski the trees

This is an environment where you need to turn fast. (You'll be surprised at how quickly you can turn when you have no choice—it's common to see intermediate skiers make expert turns in the face of a lodge pole pine.) You have to react as you ski, planning only a couple of turns in advance. Be careful, though. Tree skiing isn't the place to push your limits. Don't be ashamed to perform a controlled fall in self defense. It's far better to land on your butt in snow than on your head in wood.

A tip for skiing the trees: It is important to look at the empty places between the trees, where you want to go, and not at the trees. As humans we tend to go where we are looking.

the track
from
HOCKEY STOP
turns will be more
"Z"
shaped...

SNAP!

71 Hockey stops

One approach to making sharp quick turns is to think of doing a "hockey stop." Think of those quick stops that hockey players make, spraying ice up into the camera lens. Do that same quick twist and weighting of the skis. This speeds up the rate at which the skis cross the fall line. It also slows you down and forces the camber out of the skis. As the skis rebound at the end of the turn, use this energy to your advantage by unweighting and initiating the next turn. It should feel as though you are springing off your boards into the next turn and then aggressively weighting them.

Sometimes an exaggerated hockey-stop turn will result in that "windshield wiper" effect. The problem is that you dump speed so efficiently, you almost come to a complete halt. This produces unwanted Z-shaped tracks. This is an easy problem to correct, however; just lessen the power of that snap-twist and allow your turns to melt smoothly into each other.

SHHHH!

72 Sneaking

A simple way to collect yourself into a nice tight tele-stance is to "sneak" as you ski. It's impossible to get too spread out and wobbly if you're sneaking down the hill. Go ahead and pantomime that classic, scrunched-down cartoonish body language. Do your best to quietly tiptoe down the slopes.

73 Develop a rhythm

Skiing is a dynamic sport that demands rhythm. For some of us this rhythm comes from our pole plants. For others it is the simple up and down of weighting and unweighting. Breathing out loud with each turn is another great way to develop a rhythm. Find something that gives you a feel for doing nice even turns. Find your own rhythm.

the FALL line

74 Hands on the control panel

If you were piloting a high-performance jet fighter in combat, you wouldn't want your hands to leave the control panel. It could prove disastrous if you had to reach behind you in the cockpit for any reason. So if your pole plants are dragging your hands behind you, consider it an in-flight disaster. Snap those hands forward into the proper position on the controls. This panel is in front of you and low (in your lap). It should be pointing down the fall line. If you let it slip out from in front of you, then your aircraft is stalling in mid-flight!

75 Kicking a ball

To get that back leg to snap forward when you make the transition from one turn to the next, think about kicking a soccer ball. Don't try to send it the length of the field; a swift tap will do. If you kick the ball too hard, you straighten up your front knee, which you should keep bent. Instead of aiming the ball straight in front of you, kick it off to the side slightly in the direction of your next turn. Imagine dribbling the ball with alternate feet as you travel down the slope.

SWEEP into NEXT TURN

76 Headlights on the knees

Imagine you have a set of headlights on your knees. You point the beam in the direction of your turn as if you are steering a car. Bent knees are nice and pointy, and the "arrow" they create is directed into each turn. However, your headlights only stay attached to bent knees–if you stand up straight the lamp will pop off. So keep your knees bent and shining into each turn. If this is too much to think about, concentrate only on your back knee. Make the light from this knee sweep smoothly into each turn.

77 Unscrew a jar lid

Think of holding a jar between the knees. As you switch lead skis you alternate between screwing the lid on and off. Feel the lid as it rotates; put some pressure on it so you don't drop the jar. This helps tighten up your stance and gives a good visual image of how your knees should pass by each other during your transition between turns.

78 Your torso as a spring

Not the kind of spring that stretches up and down, but rather the type that twists back and forth. This spring has lots of energy and rebound when it is twisted. Our spine is a good example of this spring. If your upper body faces down the hill as you turn, then the action of your skis crossing the fall line will wind the spring up. Use the torque from this wound-up spring to turn your skis back the other direction. Let the spring do the work and simply allow your skis to make quick transitions from side to side.

first:
Gently hold
a PENNY between
your butt cheeks

79 Squeeze those butt cheeks

It's every tele-skier's goal to tighten up their stance. But sometimes those feet just get too far apart. To fix this, take a penny (or at least pretend to) and gently hold it between your butt cheeks. Next, squeeze those butt cheeks together and start skiing. C'mon, really work those muscles! You will notice instantly that you simply can't let those legs get spread out. As you make your turns, concentrate on not letting go of that penny.

next:
Squeeze those
BUTT CHEEKS together
while skiing
and
DON'T LET GO OF
THAT PENNY!

80 Bending modestly

Women who wear mini-skirts have a powerful advantage when perfecting their telemark stance. Trying to retain some degree of modesty while bending down with a mini-skirt on has given them the opportunity to practice exactly the type of balanced stance you need for tele-turns.

So if you are a guy and are having some trouble with the stance, try slipping on something short and tight and have a friend review your technique. Practice makes perfect.

YIN
the Transition
(UN-WEIGHTING)

YANG
the TURN!
(WEIGHTING)

81 Mystical truths revealed within the telemark turn

Look beyond the earthly limitations of the telemark turn. The duality of existence can be seen in the humble telemark skier. In the transition between turns (unweighting) the skier is reaching and expanding upward toward the heavens like a lotus flower in spring, floating beyond the limitations of gravity and heavy snow. This action is the Yin.

In the turn (weighting), every thing is reversed. Power and force contract into the dynamic warrior. Going beyond the simple compression of a turn, the warrior attacks it like a samurai in battle. This is the Yang.

The mystical truth is that the Yin and the Yang are eternally linked. One cannot exist without the other. This is the insight to skiing. You are both Yin and Yang; the transition and the turn flow into one. The unweighting gives way to the weighting and around it goes. It's cosmic.

HARD PACK
2 Dimensional skiing
(Yawn...)

Working them EDGES

82 Hard-pack vs. powder

These are as different as New Hampshire and Utah. Hard-pack (usually found at ski areas, although corn snow in the backcountry is hard-pack too) exists on a two-dimensional plane. The surface is something you stay on top of. Your turns are done by biting in with your edges, and it hurts when you fall.

Powder is another world. You are moving through a three-dimensional volume of puffy wonderfulness, side to side and up and down within the snow. It's a wonderful experience that makes you feel as if you are flying (Maybe that's why so many of us become addicted to it.) Edges serve little purpose here; instead you want to ride on your bases and use them as a platform upon which to float. Relax and bounce, bob up and down within the snow. The wider and softer the ski, the better.

Many an area skier has become discombobulated when confronted with champagne fluff for the first time. They're trapped in a two-dimensional mind set. They need to expand their comprehension into the third dimension.

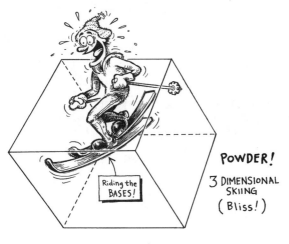

POWDER!

3 DIMENSIONAL SKIING

(Bliss!)

Riding the BASES!

83 Bounce!

Skiing the soft stuff is as much an attitude as a skill. The one skill that brings it all together is the bounce! The not-very-subtle mantra of "Boing-Boing" is exactly the mindset you want for bottomless fluff, especially with soft, wide skis. This may sound overly simplistic, but let the skis do the work. As you ski, ignore your edges and ride your bases. Find a bounce that matches the rebound of your skis. Don't try to fit the skis to a rhythm—instead, let the rhythm fit the skis! Here's a list of tips that work miracles when skiing powder:

· Relax
· Keep a quiet upper body
· Weight and un-weight
· Use the skis' rebound
· Ski the fall line
· Pretend you're on one big ski
· Don't be afraid of a little speed

It's hard to argue with any of these basics, but they are especially important in powder. Don't get spread out, because the surface area of your "one big ski" can get long and skinny, and you want to be floating on a wide platform.

84 Riding porpoises

Think what it would be like to ride on the back of a porpoise as it dives in and out of the water. These graceful animals arch back and forth as they rise up and drop back down into the water, enjoying every minute of play. If you were to ride on their backs as you skied down the fall line, you would get a sense for how your skis should move underneath you in bottomless powder: Compressing as you drop into the snow and extending as you rise back up. With springy skis you can even launch out of the snow when you're unweighting.

85 One big ski

When skiing in powder snow, think of your skis as one big platform under your feet. You are using your momentum down the hill to direct this platform in the direction you are heading. You have the advantage of being able to move your feet independent of the platform. It is important to distribute your weight carefully on this platform to avoid tipping it over. Let each motion of your body flow into the next one like liquid metal.

86 Really reach down the hill

When you are skiing on steep terrain, you need to reach down-hill to keep the weight over your skis. Think about reaching down with your pole and leaning your upper body down into the next turn. The steeper the terrain, the more aggressive you need to be when reaching down for that pole plant.

87 Keep both hands in your field of view

This is a good thing to be doing at all times, but it's incredibly key when skiing in steep terrain. If you can't see your hands, it means they must be somewhere behind you. You want your hands to be out in front, helping you face the fall line, and moving you downhill. The downhill hand will not be the problem—if you are doing downhill pole plants like you should be. It is usually the pesky hand that just did a pole plant that gets left behind. Think about reaching it across your body (downhill) so you can see it.

88 Jump turns

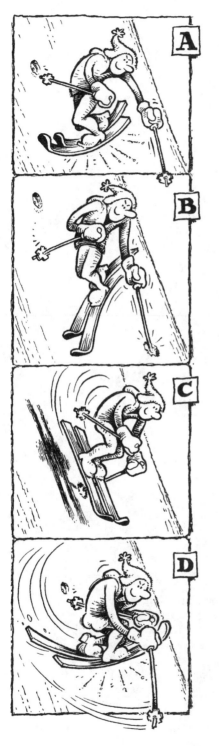

In a jump turn, you are literally jumping off your skis to become airborne, and then switching leads and direction while you are in the air to land back on the snow in mid-turn. Think about down-weighting your skis really hard (so that they will spring back hard and help you get airborne) and then jumping off them with both feet. While in the air, drop your front foot back—it needs to be the back foot when you land, and this is faster than moving the back foot forward. Land and compress hard again to start your next turn.

89 Keep your hip away from the slope

Do whatever it takes to keep your uphill hip as far away as you can from the slope behind you. Your hips are connected to your spine and legs, enabling you to move and rotate them into some extreme positions. Imagine you have a flat holographic plane around your hips; this will make it easier to visualize the body positions you need to achieve. First, create distance from your hip and the slope by angling your pelvis down the hill. Second, get some more distance by rotating your hips around so that they are facing downhill. Third, get even more distance by leaning down the hill, bending at your hip.

You want to have your body (or at least your butt) over your skis in order to weight them. If you don't get that weight over them, they will slide out from under you, causing you to fall on your butt.

the UPHILL HIP

THE FALL LINE

HOLOGRAPHIC HIP PLANE!

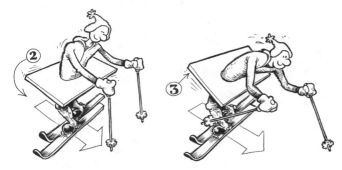

90 Skiing breakable crud

This can be miserable. You can't be dainty, you have to be aggressive and attack the crud 500-lb. gorilla style. Hunker down low and punch through with each turn. Unweight aggressively and turn your skis as they leave the snow.

91 Lots of ski length

One of the advantages of the telemark position is that your "one big ski" platform is so much longer than either of your skis. This length can be wonderfully stable in cruddy snow. Take advantage of all that distance between the tip of your front ski and the tail of your back ski. You can use that skiable surface to ride (or bash through) some less-than-perfect snow. Plus, the stability of the "long ski" is enhanced because you need to get low in order to make that platform good and long. You can really use this long platform to your advantage when you're speeding down a narrow track and are suddenly confronted with a sizable dip in the trail. The long platform can be used to really absorb the energy that might unhinge skiers who keep their feet together and ride on a short platform.

LOTSA LENGTH in the SKI-ABLE SURFACE

92 Don't be afraid of a little speed

Airplanes need speed on the runway before they can fly. Are you like an airplane putt-putting down the runway at a miserable crawl? If so, you'll never fly. Those skis need to move before they can blossom into the amazing tools that make skiing so much fun. Don't fight it, let them rip! With a little speed they'll float and bounce, and turning them will be less work. Use that momentum to get those skis flying.

Tips 93 through 109 are common
Mistakes
(and how to fix them!)

93 Don't get frustrated

When things are not going your way it's time to stop and regroup. Frustration is the worst possible state of mind to be in. Tell yourself to relax; imagine succeeding with just one aspect of your turn instead of trying to get it all right. If this still doesn't work, call it a day and try again later. Remember that learning is a life-long process and it's good for the soul to start all over again, if only for the sake of humility. Skiing is fun, and something has gone wrong if you can't keep that in mind. *See Tips 51, 52, 55, and 58.*

94 Double pole plants

There are excellent skiers who make perfect-looking double pole plants, and if that's your style, go for it. But if you are double-poling by default, or because you feel off balance, then it's time to work on that single downhill pole plant. That's what will ultimately improve your skiing. *See Tips 37, 38, 39, and 41.*

95 Don't use your uphill pole as a point of balance

If you find yourself doing uphill pole plants then stop it. This is a bad habit to get into. It means you are leaning into the hill, when what you really want is to be leaning down the hill and planting that pole down there as well. Don't be afraid of what's below you. Trust yourself and lean downhill. *See Tips 37, 38, 39, 41, 45, and 66.*

96 Spidering

Do you find that you can't ski down the hill without the support of your poles? If so, then what you need to work on is your balance while moving. The best way to do this is to spend more time on skis. Get comfortable schussing along. *See Tips 10, 62, and 66.*

97 Don't drag your uphill pole

This can be an anchor keeping you from facing the fall line and thus unable to initiate quick turns. Think about keeping those hands in front of you and facing downhill. *See Tips 38, 39, 41, 74, 86, and 87.*

Too spread out

Yikes! I would hate to fall like this. Work on getting a tighter stance. Being spread out reduces your ability to properly weight your skis. It also keeps you from using your legs as shock absorbers and springs for unweighting into your next turn. *See tips 15,20,61,72,77.*

 Bend that front leg

This is a common mistake. It is important to bend that front leg. It gives you a tighter stance and allows you to absorb whatever the snow surface may throw at you. Have a friend watch you. If you are skiing straight-legged, go back to easier terrain where you can concentrate on skiing in good form. Work on that muscle memory so you don't need to think about it. You should be able to feel the pressure of the tongue of your boot against your shin. *See Tips 6, 22, 76, 80.*

100 Crossed skis

Some times when you hunker down for that low tele-turn you stand up and find your skis are crossed! You made two mistakes. First you got too spread out, enough to let that ski tip sneak behind your boot. Second, the back ski wasn't weighted enough and wobbled out of its track. To correct this, stand tighter and weight that back ski more.

Believe it or not, you can still complete a rather "elegant" wedge-like turn in this pretzel pose. You can even sink into the next turn and actually un-cross them (short skis help) with nary a pause in your rhythm. *See Tips 20, 30, 61, 72, 77, and 79.*

101 Don't freeze into the tele-position

The telemark turn is a dynamic turn. You should always be in motion, either sinking down into the turn or rising up out of it. If you are making really wide turns and long traverses, then it means you're stuck in the tele-position too long. It's as if your brain synapses have momentarily stopped firing. Think about sinking into the turn and then rising up into the next as one fluid motion. *See Tips 25, 27, 34, 58, 63, 65, 69, and 92.*

102 Unequal weight on the skis

If you don't weight those skis correctly, they will never do what you want them to. If you don't get enough weight on the back ski, then it is squirrelly and you frequently wind up with crossed skis. If you have all that weight on the back ski however, then you won't have control of the front ski. This last scenario happens to people in steep terrain who are afraid to commit to the fall line. Get that weight over the ski by reaching down the fall line. *See Tips 28, 30, 67, 85, 86, and 89.*

103 Falling backward

If this fall looks familiar, you are making a couple mistakes that are conspiring to land you in the snow. This skier is only weighting his front ski. He then makes it even more awkward by letting his body get too far behind the ski. This combination simply doesn't work.

Think of that back leg as a balloon. Your body is positioned over it, and your front leg has been desperately supporting all your weight. You lean back and "pop," you end up deflating the back leg. You need to use that back leg for support instead of just trailing it behind you.

Correct this by doing two things. One, keep your upper body down the hill and over your front ski. Two, weight both skis evenly by keeping a tighter stance so that your back leg is not trailing uselessly. *See Tips 28, 30, 45, 47 and 67.*

(104) Back ski tip dives

With the age of plastic boots this problem is show-
ing up more and more with hard pack skiers who are venturing
into soft snow for the first time. The toe baffle and sole on
plastic boots can be so stiff that if you don't get enough weight
on the back ski, the boot causes the tip to dive—and down you
go in a half-pirouette. You need to weight that ski and use a
tight stance that keeps the heel closer to the ski. This problem
is rare with floppy leather boots; they are simply too soft. Not
enough weight on the back ski with leathers usually results in
crossed skis or, if the front ski dives, a head plant. *See Tips 30
and 85.*

TURN!

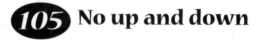

TRANSITION

SWISH!

TURN!

105 No up and down

If you are making the transition between turns without extending and compressing your legs, your skiing is missing something. Your skis are designed to rebound and help you unweight. If you don't take advantage of this by extending and compressing, you are working harder then you need to. Staying low will keep you stable, but a little up and down (extension and compression) will help you take advantage of your skis' built in camber. *See Tips 10, 27, 29, and 33.*

INVOLUNTARY
PARALLEL
STANCE
MID-TELE-TURN!

106 Sneaky parallel turn

Many lifelong alpine skiers will make this mistake. The parallel turn is a fallback position that can involuntarily sneak itself into your tele-skiing, appearing in some strange places. Often you won't even know you're doing this—it takes someone watching you to point it out. It may manifest itself as a tele-turn in which only the inside edge of the downhill ski is weighted.

You may have put years of time and effort into creating some parallel turn muscle memory, and those habits are hard to break. The mistake is fundamental; it's a lack of trust in the tele-position, and lack of the proper muscle memory. You need to give yourself over to the tele-turn; nothing less than complete commitment will do. *See Tips 6, 11, 18, 19, 30, and 77.*

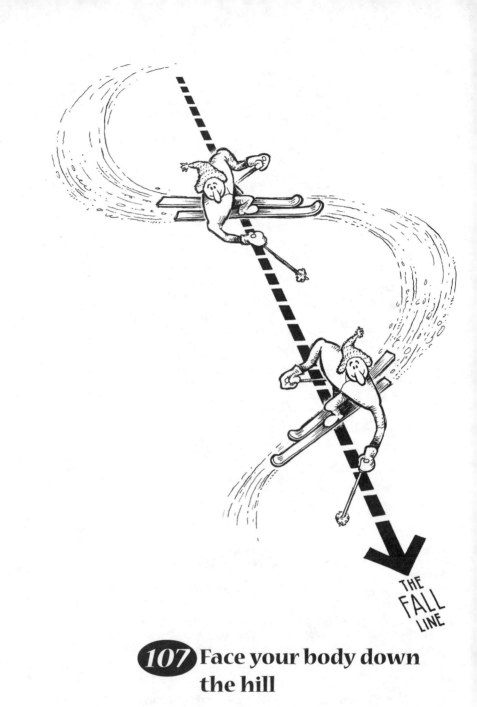

THE FALL LINE

107 Face your body down the hill

This poor guy is riding his skis the way you would push a grocery cart. While he may be looking down the hill, his torso and hips are facing across the fall line, just like his skis. You want your whole upper body facing down the fall line. *See Tips 21, 34, 35, 37, 43, 45, and 50.*

108 Use caution when teaching your significant other to ski

Maybe this isn't a problem for you, but things have gotten heated on the slopes between couples more than once. Since we live in a more enlightened age, it is often hard for couples who are used to relating to one another on an equal basis to suddenly accept the roles of teacher and student. Sometimes it's just cheaper and more sane to pay someone else for those lessons.

109 Don't think about all these tips at once

It's far too overwhelming to think about all these tips at once. Don't swamp your mind with every trick in the book; just find that one tip that makes the most sense to you and work on it until it comes naturally. Then go back and find the next tip. Its like building a house. You can only lay one brick at a time.

Good luck!

AUTHORS

Allen O'Bannon grew up in Portland, Oregon and first learned to ski on the slopes of Mount Hood. In the mid-80s he made not only a transition to the mountains of the west but also to a pair of freeheel bindings. Allen has worked for the National Outdoor Leadership School since 1987 and is a senior instructor in the NOLS winter program. Unable to find a real job, he turned to writing this book to support his ski habit. He currently resides for part of the year in Victor, Idaho and is planning a presidential campaign for 2004.

Mike Clelland never went to Art School, studying Mad Magazine instead. Mike grew up in the flat plains of Michigan, then spent ten years (as a Yuppie!) in New York City. In 1987 he thought it might be fun to be a ski bum in Wyoming for the winter. Unfortunately, after living and skiing in the Rockies, he found it quite impossible to return to his previous life in the Big City. Mike is presently living in a shed in Idaho where he divides his time between illustrator and NOLS instructor.